# The Job Delusion

Think your way to financial freedom!

## Kevin H. Boyd

*A catalogue record for this book is available from the British Library*

Front cover:
Designed by Toby Moore 2023

Published by Kevin H. Boyd

www.kevinhboyd.com


Audio book version available on Audible

https://www.audible.co.uk/pd/The-Job-Delusion-Audiobook/B00XRGSZY2

I dedicate this book to all my teachers that guided
me on the path to financially freedom.

Special mention must go to Toby M., Lucy B.,
Ariana G. and Edward H. who inspired, encouraged
and pointed out with compassion when I was deluding
myself.

I wrote this book so that my son, Simon, will inherit
not just my wealth but the mind-set that created it.

# Genesis

Kevin H. Boyd – Brighton, UK - 2023

**Kevin H. Boyd** was born in 1965 in Stevenston, Ayrshire, a small working-class town on the west coast of Scotland. He was born to Kay & Jim with a cleft-pallet and a hair-lip, and spent his early years having this unique feature pointed out to him on a regular basis which helped him realise he would never be popular or follow group think in his life. This was a great gift to be given to him by his fellow Scotsmen.

At age 19, Kevin eventually escaped Scotland and headed south to the cultural hub that is Brighton, on the south coast of England and started a new life as a computer programmer in the emerging world of *digital media*.

Kevin is also father to Simon, who he hopes, one day, will set the world alight with his own creative vision and entrepreneurial spirit.

Kevin has spent most of his life trying to figure out a better, smarter and more creative way to be in the world and this book is his attempt to gift what he has learned to you.

# Commitment

*"Until one is committed, there is hesitancy, the chance to draw back. Concerning all acts of initiative (and creation), there is one elementary truth that ignorance of which kills countless ideas and splendid plans: that the moment one definitely commits oneself, then Providence moves too. All sorts of things occur to help one that would never otherwise have occurred.*

*A whole stream of events issues from the decision, raising in one's favour all manner of unforeseen incidents and meetings and material assistance, which no man could have dreamed would have come his way.*

*Whatever you can do, or dream you can do, begin it. Boldness has genius, power, and magic in it. Begin it now."*

**Scottish mountaineer William Hutchinson Murray, 1951 (drawing on <u>Goethe</u>)**

## Why, yet another get-rich-quick book?

There are hundreds of those evangelical **get-rich-quick** books on the bestsellers lists.

Why does the world need another one?

Whenever I read one of those, **here is how easily I got rich** biographies, by some self-made millionaire, I was always left with the feelings of both envy and inadequacy that I would never get rich quick or even slowly!

That *belief* was like having my foot pressed firmly on the brake on my journey through life and was one of the many excuses I used to avoid taking action to improve my life.

But eventually I realised, that doubting voice was just a *limiting belief* (See Chapter 2), something that had been subtly programmed into me throughout my early life.

To take my foot off the brake, I was going to have to understand *why* I limited myself with these beliefs and *where* had I got them from?

So, what where my earliest memories of having money?

**Money is whatever your parents/friends/teachers/media told you it was.**

My earliest memory of having *money* was when I was about 8 years old; every week my parents gave me 30 pence pocket money (£3 in 2023) and I would excitedly insert each shiny ten pence piece into a transparent sepia coloured piggy bank that the local bank branch had given my parents to encourage us kids to save. And each week those sepia-tinged ten pence coins would grow into a treasure chest of potential that **I just couldn't wait to spend!**

I see now that my childhood experiences of money where:

*"Save just enough money to buy what you want and then spend it immediately for instant gratification!"*

And this saving pattern would rule me for the first 40 years of my life!

In Western culture we call this **saving,** but it is in fact really just a form of *delayed* consumerism. We save for a short period of time and then we spend it; there is no real *saving,* let alone, *investing* going on.

Then once I had spent my savings, I would experience **buyer's regret**, the feelings of loss and shame at no longer having the potential of growing my small hill of coins into a mountain of wealth. I had not learned to be a financial mountaineer; instead, all I had learned was how to stay at base camp and look up at the peak in disbelief that I could ever get there.

## A good education is the way to prosperity, isn't it?

When I left school in 1981 at age 16, with five mediocre **O-Grade** (Scottish version of GCSE) exam passes to my name, I was told by my parents that if I was to get a *good job* then I would need to go to university and study more. Even though it was quite evident to us both that academia and I did not get on.

But my parents believed that further education was the gateway to a better job and therefore a better life. That approach had helped them in the 1950s become socially mobile, moving from a poor working-class upbringing to a more comfortable middle-class life.

So, despite my misgivings, I reluctantly went off to university for three years, fully paid for by the government, to study the newly emerging world of computer programming.

As at school, I was soon disillusioned and bored at university with the dry teachings about how a computer worked and drawing flowcharts of business processes.

So, to escape the boredom, I started writing simple 8-Bit video games for the newly emerging **home computer** market of the early 1980s.

During this period, I created around a dozen or so games that were published in UK home computer magazines.

Back before the internet and downloads, people had to type in hundreds of lines of computer code, just to play one of these basic 8-bit games. I was probably the only student in university to end his three years of study with more money in the bank than when I started!

But this early entrepreneurial venture soon withered on the vine as none of my university teachers had considered it helpful to teach me how to setup and grow a business from scratch, it was all about preparing me to have a *job*!

### The Tyranny – my first ever job

When I graduated from university in 1984, the UK was in a deep economic recession caused by trying to tame double-digit inflation while grappling with the profound changes of globalisation forcing most of the UKs manufacturing base to relocate to east Asia.

This meant I had to migrate 700 miles from my home town in Scotland down to the south of England. It was an early lesson in the brutality of the **exchanging your time for money** model, that forced me to leave my friends and family behind, just to have a *job!*

My first job was very much at the cutting edge of technology, building hardware and software to make video interactive, using 12-inch analogue videodiscs that only held 30-minutes of content.

I worked day and night for three years for some very large clients but by the end of it all I was totally burnt-out and was ready to quit. I was frustrated to have built some ground breaking products with very little to show for it, other than making my boss richer, and he didn't even pay me overtime or give me shares in the company for all that innovative work!

So, in 1988, at the age of just twenty-two, I quit my job in disgust, sold everything I owned and went off backpacking around the world in search of a better way to live.

## The Exodus – into the desert

When you leave a tyranny you don't go straight to the land of milk and honey, first you must spend time in the desert.

My time in the desert consisted of hitch-hiking around western Europe, spending hours standing by the side of the road with my sign held out pleading with drivers to take me to the next town. When I arrived, I would have to stay in crowded hostels and begin searching for work. And not speaking the local language meant I was offered the most menial of jobs, like dish washing in a hotel kitchen, picking up turkey eggs on a factory farm or picking fruit in orchards.

Not quite the promised land I had hoped for.

## Wherever you go, you take the weather with you

After three years of doing menial jobs all around the world I found myself sitting on Bondi beach in Sydney, Australia watching the surfers ride in on top of the waves and thought *"I'm in the promised land, I should feel happy now"*, but I didn't!

Instead, I felt that even though it had been great fun backpacking around the world, doing the odd temp job here and there to fund my travels, what was now missing from my life was a sense of **purpose and meaning**, of actually being useful to other people and I really missed having a *professional* career.

## Back to the day job

In early 1991, just as Tim Berners-Lee was hooking up the first World Wide Web page to the Internet, I returned to England to get back on the career ladder in the exciting world of nineties **Information Technology**.

But this time I was going to be way smarter, this time I would **be my own boss!** So, I became a *freelancer*, sounded good but turned out that now I had the extra burden of being the marketing, accounts and debt recovery departments, as well as doing the actual job!

But, as the years ticked by, I found I got caught in an endless cycle of working for as short a period as I could tolerate, to recover from being broke, and then avoiding work and doing more fun things like studying

Buddhism and psychology, until poverty drove me back to my next freelance contract.

I tolerated this push-pull cycle of **The Job Delusion** for another decade-and-a-half, until I turned forty.

## The straw that broke the camel's back

In 2006, I was working for a particularly demanding client who neither understood the discipline of software development nor cared how much extra work he was creating for me every time he changed his mind. I was complaining to my friend and coach, Ariana, about how little money I was making from yet another freelance contract.

Ariana, looked at me with a sympathetic eye and said, *"There are other ways to make a living in life."* *"What do you mean?"*, I asked.

She then told me about a seminar she had recently attended that had shown her how she could create **passive income** in her life by buying rental properties. Passive income? What a concept, I was intrigued. So, after a bit more persuasion by Ariana and other property investor friends, I eventually took my sceptical mind off to a free seminar at a local airport conference hall to have my mind blown and of course to eat the free lunch they put on!

## If you always do what you've always done...

They say the biggest part of our knowledge is the bit we **don't know** and so it is always best to enter a new field with a **beginner's mind** and be fully open to learning new ideas. But I went along with a mindset of **knowing better** and sure in my belief that they wouldn't persuade me to invest in property; I was way smarter than that!

As I sat there in the conference hall with my name badge stuck to my chest and scribbled in magic marker pen, I had a revelation. It became clear that I was missing out on a technique that could provide greater freedom in my life.

I had always believed that the increased value in my home, it's equity, was just a number that meant nothing until the day I sold it.

But the conference speaker pointed out that I could in fact take nearly all of this extra value, around 85% of the **equity,** this frozen money in my home, and **leverage it** via a re-mortgage. No need to sell it, I could continue to live in it and use the leveraged money to invest in even more property that could provide an income for the rest of my days!

Wow, as I physically and mentally skipped-out of that conference room, I was burning with desire to know much more about how to build passive income and see Chapter 6 for details of how I did.

## The hardest part of any journey is taking that first step

That one powerful insight, of **using the equity in my own home to buy more property**, was the beginning of my journey towards financial freedom.

I started reading the classic texts on becoming wealthy and attended over-hyped workshops on how to **become a millionaire overnight** by some of the world's most famous wealth gurus like **Anthony Robbins, T. Harv Eker** and **Robert Kiyosaki** who jet around the world **selling dreams to dreamers**, for hundreds and sometimes thousands of pounds (more in Chapter 3 about that).

Even though these evangelical wealth gurus took far more of my money than I would have liked, what they taught me started to slowly get me past my old limiting beliefs. That I could see that there was another way to create money in my life that didn't involve just exchanging my time for money in a job for the rest of my days.

So, I wrote this book to remind myself of what I have learnt and most of all, dear reader, to help you to wake up to **The Job Delusion** – the idea that exchanging your time for money is the smartest way to provide for you and your family for the rest of your life.

## Keeping it short and to the point

I've kept the book short because, to my mind, too many self-help books ramble on and on about the same point.

Knowing your time is precious I've kept each chapter to the bare minimum; if you want to delve deeper into the subjects covered in the chapters there are links to websites and books to enable you to deepen your knowledge.

So, let's begin by looking at how we think...

# PART 1

~

## Thinking

*"The roots produce the fruits"*

**T. Harv Eker**

# The Job Delusion

*"A delusion is a belief held with strong conviction, despite superior evidence."* – Wikipedia

The *delusion* that I inherited from my family, teachers, and community was:

*1. Study hard at school, get good grades, and you will be allowed to go to university.*

*2. If you study hard at university and get the best degree possible, you will have the honour of applying for your first job.*

*3. If you sacrifice yourself at your job long enough, hopefully, your boss will promote you up the corporate ladder, increasing your salary and pension as you climb.*

*4. If you keep working for, say, fifty years, then when you retire at age seventy, you will finally have enough time and money to do all the things you couldn't do because you were working so hard at a job you hated.*

So, what is wrong with that? After all, it worked for my parents!

To understand why it worked for my parents but was not going to work for you and me, we first need to brush up on some economic history...

## A brief history of Western capitalism

My parents were born in 1936 and 1940 and so they lived through a unique period in our Western economy; they were the generation that grew up through the Second World War and became the baby boomers. It was Western capitalism's golden era and the people of Western Europe and North America experienced unprecedented increases in their standard of living, many times that of their parents.

After 1945, a new social contract was agreed between the workers and the political classes. This contract essentially said that the government would look after you throughout your life. So, if you could not find a job or grew too sick or old then the government would look after you.

When I was going through my formative education, in the 1970s and early 1980s, I felt no need to learn about creating wealth for myself and neither did the education system feel I needed to know either. The assumption was that there would always be a well-paid job available to me and if not, then the government would look after me until there was.

What I was not aware of was that as I lived through the last three decades of the twentieth century the governments and the corporations of the West were giving away nearly all of their manufacturing base to Asia and South America, so that these corporations could maximise their profits and their CEOs could take huge bonuses for their genius cost cutting work.

These newly emerging industrial nations ended up with so much money that they started to lend it back to us, at very low rates. Credit became so cheap in the West that this discouraged most us from saving and instead we spent it on all the new cheaply manufactured goods that were flooding into our countries. And so when we ran out of our own money we just borrowed even more from our ever-so-responsible banking system that encouraged us to borrow many times our income on credit cards, loans and mortgages. What could possibly go wrong with that?

## Whoops

In 2008 the system finally collapsed under the weight of all that debt, the banks went bust and we in the West woke up to the fact that the party was over. The social contract could not be fulfilled anymore; the government had no money left to pay for all the goodies they had promised us every time an election came around. In fact, they really needed us to give them even more of our money to pay off the debt they had run up; over a **trillion pounds** in the UK alone in 2010.

Check out _Whoops_ by John Lanchester for a more detailed insight into what happened in 2008

The Western governments also told us all that we now needed to produce more, export more, and be more entrepreneurial. We needed to grow our way out of this recession.

So, how was I going to generate more income in my life? Unfortunately, the British education system had not taught me anything about how to build a business or even how to invest my money, so that it worked harder and smarter for me and the country.

Like the rest of the working and middle classes I had just spent everything I ever earned, and as soon as I got a pay rise I would go out and buy a bigger house, a bigger car and ultimately build a bigger debt pile.

Ironically, when the bank offers you a credit card, it is really offering you more debt. So, a *credit card* should now really be called a *debt card*.

## Own assets not liabilities

I now wanted really practical tips on how to become wealthy. So, I headed over to Amazon.co.uk and searched for books about wealth creation and I found 7,717 search results.

Hard to believe so much had been written about the subject and yet so few of us know much about it!

I narrowed my search first down to just Personal Finance and then down to Investing, which resulted in a more manageable 88 books.

As I scrolled through the list an interesting title caught my eye: *Rich Dad Poor Dad* by Robert Kiyosaki.

Kiyosaki makes a fundamental point that an **Asset** is something that brings money to you and a **Liability** is something that takes money from you.

For most of us, even our own home takes money from us, usually in the form of a mortgage, council tax, insurance and maintenance. The same is true of our other favourite big purchase in life, our cars.

A major concept I took away from Kiyosaki's book was that you need to aim at acquiring assets that pay you money every day of your life, even when you are on holiday! This is one of the cornerstones to becoming *financially free*.

## JOB – Just Over Broke

Kiyosaki also argues that having a job puts you at a great disadvantage as you are lulled into a false sense of security that you will always be able to **exchange your time for money** and the amount you get will always be just enough to make your life work.

However, in practice, most people end up spending more than they earn and start to run up more and more personal debt on credit cards; they also remortgage their homes, not to leverage the money released to buy more property, but to spend it on more consumer goods, on more liabilities.

The global recession of 2008 taught us all that even the most secure professional job can disappear overnight, and that your own home can be taken away from you within a few months of missing a few mortgage payments.

So, is having a job really **the safe option**?

## Cashflow Quadrant

In Kiyosaki's next book *The Cashflow Quadrant* he breaks down the key ways that most of us make our money into four quadrants.

| Employee | Business Owner |
|---|---|
| You have a job | You own a system and people work for you |
| Self-employed | Investor |
| You own a job | Money works for you |

Most of us spend our lives on the left side of the quadrant by having a job or being self-employed. I had spent 15 years being self-employed and so when I read Kiyosaki's delusion busting idea that being self-employed was just the same as having a job, except now you also get the extra headaches of running your company too, I was shocked. I realised that I had not been any smarter than someone with a regular job; I too had **The Job Delusion.**

## The Right side is where the wealth is.

The right side of the quadrant is where the wealthy spend their time, either owning a business or owning investments that generate money even when they are not there, in other words **Passive Income**.

Now, which quadrant you feel most comfortable in depends on your *core values*. These were formed in you by your parents, teachers and friends. I came from a working-class background and so I had been programmed to just have a job for the rest of my life. The thought of running my own business or investing money in assets was quite an alien concept.

Working on the right side of the quadrant is also a lot more tax efficient, as when you have a job you are taxed first and then you get to spend what is left. But when you own a business you can spend some of that profit on your own needs like education and travel first, and then get taxed on what's left.

## Your net worth is not just cash

Kiyosaki goes on to define wealth, not just in money terms, but in how many days you could live without a job and still maintain your standard of living. It brings home the fundamental point that it is not how much money you **earn** each month but how much of it you **keep**.

I calculated how long I could survive without working and was disturbed to see that after only 3 months I would be broke and soon homeless due to being unable to pay my mortgage on my biggest liability of all, my own home. I was self-employed, so if I got sick and could not work I would be in big trouble in just 3 months. I couldn't carry on living like that with no safety net; it was time to change how I made money and more importantly how my money worked for me.

## Think like the rich

After reading both of Kiyosaki's books I was now getting much clearer on what I had to **DO** to **HAVE** wealth, but the real key to my future success was how I needed to **BE**. If I wanted to be rich, I had to start thinking like someone who had money, not like everyone else around me who were just as stuck in the *exchanging their time for money* delusion as I was.

But I had to be honest with myself as my mind was full of *limiting beliefs* about how I could ever achieve any form of financial freedom.

The harsh reality of my life was that I had been subtly trained by society to just have a job; that it was too risky to invest my money or start up my own business and become an entrepreneur.

It was clear to me that the first thing I needed to do was change the way I thought about myself and wealth, as I was starting to realise that I was actually taking a giant risk with my future by taking **no risk at all**!

# Limiting beliefs

*"He who looks outside his own heart dreams, he who looks inside his own heart awakens."* – Carl Jung

## What are limiting beliefs?

A limiting belief is something that you believe is true about yourself, other people, or the world. Whether it would stand up to scientific analysis does not matter; the fact you *believe* it is good enough for your mind to subtly affect your daily actions.

It forms part of your *narrative*, the story you tell yourself about who you are and how the world is.

We are **meaning creation machines**. We attach meaning to almost everything that happens to us in our lives.

*"I'm poor because I did not get good grades at school."*

*"I tried once before to be rich and failed so it is not meant to be."*

*"I don't have to try hard to be successful as the Universe/God/Destiny will provide."*

You then invest a lot of energy and selective fact-finding into writing your story and how you, the hero, play your role. Your story contains all of your limiting beliefs that subtly control your thoughts, your feelings, and, most importantly, your actions, for the rest of your life.

So, if you believe you are **not smart enough to become successful** then, when you see a job advertised, that you are capable of doing, your limiting beliefs will stop you from even applying for it. And that is subtly how limiting beliefs control the destiny of our lives.

When your thoughts are saying **I can't do that**, and you know another human being has done it before, then that's a limiting belief.

In Daniel Goleman's book *Emotional Intelligence* he refers to research that shows that most CEOs of large companies have a lower IQ than most of their employees. But what these CEOs do have is high emotional intelligence to manage their moods, relate well in social groups and to take action despite the fear and uncertainty often felt by their employees. In other words, they are in control of their thoughts and feelings; this is what makes them successful, not being the smartest or riches person in the room!

This revelation helped me see that I had some strong limiting beliefs ingrained in me by the incredibly poor state education system I had been subjected to as a child back in the UK education system. In the twentieth century educators where focused more on you learning facts and skills that employers needed instead of encouraging people to actually truly learn and create.

Current educational research demonstrates that the more mistakes we make the better we learn. But I was not in school anymore, there was no exam to sit, no A* for a teacher to award me for following the rules. It was time to challenge my limiting beliefs, embrace failure and aim for the stars.

*Hmm, how exactly do you change your limiting beliefs?*

### First define the problem.

To find a solution to a problem you first need to properly define what the problem is. What are the thoughts and beliefs that are running your life? It can be very hard to identify them in a normal rational frame of mind; so much is buried deep within our unconscious mind.

I needed to find a way to access and understand my thoughts both conscious and unconscious. They say the human mind hasn't evolved much in the last forty thousand years, and modern psychology has been investigating the mind for just the last few centuries, so surely there must be a well-documented approach to accessing the unconscious mind by now?

**The talking cure**

Back in the 1990s I had worked on discovering my back story through various different talking cures such as Counselling, Psychotherapy and even Art Therapy. At the time I had found it very helpful to get clear about my early childhood experiences and how they had affected my adult life. If you are *unfamiliar* with your own back story I would recommend at least some time spent exploring your past with the support of one of the established talking cures like Psychotherapy, as it will reveal a lot about why your present life is the way it is.

But years on from all of that exploration I was still left with a whole bunch of limiting beliefs and so I was keen to try a more practical approach to changing my behaviour.

## An ancient approach

The Buddhist tradition has recommended meditation as a technique to get to know one's mind for thousands of years. It occurred to me that a system that has taken that long to develop and mature, and that has about half a billion followers around the world, must be a good place to start.

So, I went along to a meditation class at my local Buddhist centre in Brighton and learned several meditation techniques, which helped me notice and challenge my limiting beliefs.

Here is a simple meditation technique that I found very helpful in identifying my thoughts.

### A Simple Breathing Meditation
What follows is a simple breathing meditation taken from the website how-to-meditate.org.

Sit in a comfortable chair and allow yourself 5 to 10 minutes to do this meditation:

*The purpose of meditation is to stop distractions and make our mind clearer and more lucid. This can be accomplished by practising a simple breathing meditation. Choose a quiet place to meditate and sit in a comfortable position. The most important thing is to keep your back straight to prevent your mind from becoming sluggish or sleepy.*

*Sit with your eyes closed and turn your attention to your breathing. Breathe naturally, preferably through your nostrils, without attempting to control your breath, and try to become aware of the sensation of your breath as it enters and leaves your nostrils. The sensation of the air passing in and out of your nostrils is where you want to put your attention. If you mind gets caught up in other thoughts, just notice this and gently bring yourself back to the sensation of your breath entering and leaving your nostrils.*

*At first, your mind will be very busy, and you might even feel that the meditation is making your mind busier; but in reality you are just becoming more aware of how busy your mind actually is. There will be a great temptation to follow your different thoughts as they arise, but you should resist this and just notice them and then let them float away like a bubble in the wind. When you come out of the meditation you can note down some of these thoughts but for now remain focused on the sensation of the breath. If you discover that your mind has wandered and is following your thoughts, gently return to the sensation of your breath.*

## Meditation is like exercising a muscle

At first your meditation muscle will be weak and you won't be able to go for very long, but with regular practice your meditation muscle will grow stronger and slowly but surely you will be able to meditate for longer. I reached up to an hour on some sitting, but mainly around 10-20 minutes was my norm.

One of the cool things about meditation is that it is a tool you always have with you and so can use at any point in your day, whenever you need to calm your mind and focus your thoughts. My favourite place to use it is whilst standing in a queue; it takes away my impatience and makes the chore of queuing a much more calming experience.


## My Limiting Beliefs about Money

While meditating I would often ask myself the question "How would my life be if I were rich?" and from out of my minds unconscious depths came a series of limiting beliefs about being successful and especially about money:

- It's too hard to be really successful.

- I'm not smart enough to be rich.

- I will have to change so much to be successful and I may lose who I really am!

- The love of money is the root of all evil.

- No one will like me when I'm rich.

- You can't be rich and spiritual.

- Money doesn't buy you happiness.

I realised that I had **inherited** most of these beliefs, they were second-hand ideas I had picked up from my community whilst growing up. If I was honest, I really had no idea if these beliefs were true at all?

I felt now was definitely the time to challenge these beliefs and to start experimenting with a different set of beliefs and see how my life would improve.

*If not now, then when!*

But, how exactly do I change a lifetime of conditioning?

I needed to find a technique to change my limiting beliefs as the old saying goes:

*"Insanity is repeating the same mistakes over and over again, hoping for a different result."*

So, it was time to stop the insanity and start a new way of being.

As I had been brought up in the British Socialist model, knowledge about how to make money and how to be successful had not been taught to me by the state education system or by my friends and peers. I felt that if I was going to break out of my limiting beliefs about money then I needed someone from the **American Capitalist School of thinking** to show me how!

**I am my only limitation**

Through the years I'd heard of Tony Robbins, the larger than life success guru who motivates an entire stadium full of people to walk over hot coals to demonstrate the power of overcoming limiting beliefs.

In clicking over to TonyRobbins.com and searching through his many offerings, I eventually chose Personal Power II, a 30 day programme that promised to change my limiting beliefs. Each day I listened to a 30 to 60 minute mix of stories, ideas and techniques designed to change my limiting beliefs.

Tony argues that if you don't have enough money in your life then you have not **conditioned** yourself for wealth. The theory goes like this; everybody is driven by two primal forces:

1. Their need to avoid **pain**.

2. Their desire to gain **pleasure**.

We want to move away from **pain** and move towards **pleasure**. Most of us feel pain around the idea of having more money than we need, and putting the effort required into achieving it. It is much more pleasurable to stay in our **comfort zone** as that doesn't require any effort to change.

When I used to think about how much effort and hard work would be involved in being rich it was just too *painful* for me to even contemplate. I needed to change my conditioning because every action I took towards changing was being subtly undermined by the desire to avoid pain. It was like adjusting the rudder on my ship of life a fraction every day. It was not obvious on a day-to-day basis but as I approached 40 I realised that my direction of travel was way off target. I wanted to be sitting on a beach sipping Piña Coladas not slogging away as an *IT-droid* for the rest of my life!

## Anchoring

Tony's main tool to enable change was to use Anchoring, which is a technique developed by the founders of Neuro-Linguistic Programming. This is where we associate a particular feeling or thought with either, say, a touch or a particular word we hear or even a symbol we see.

To create a new association in your mind:

- First close your eyes and visualise something you love doing, something you are really successful at, and project this image onto a cinema screen in your mind's eye.

- Next zoom into the screen so the image is as large as possible.

- Now enhance the colours on the screen so they are as vivid as possible and the sound is full-on surround sound and loud, like you are watching an IMAX movie!

- Then really feel the positive emotions associated with this image and turn them all the way up to eleven.

- Now associate those positive feelings with the new thing that you would like to be good at but currently associate with pain.

- To help **anchor** this feeling create a word or phrase which you can use in the future to remind you of this feeling. For example, **I have a millionaire mindset.** Or, alternatively, use a physical gesture like squeezing your index finger or wearing a rubber band around your wrist and pinging it to remind you of the moment when you felt fully alive.

- Maintain this visualisation for at least 30 seconds to help build up new neural pathways in the brain.

- As **repetition is the mother of skill**, repeat this exercise every day until it is firmly anchored in your mind. Then all you have to do is say **I have a millionaire mind**, or squeeze your index finger, or ping your rubber band, and you will feel the pleasurable emotions associated with this new thought.

I must admit, the whole approach sounded rather too simplistic to change my long-held beliefs, but I did want to change my old unhelpful patterns and start to live a different life. So, I focused my mind on the pain of staying stuck in my rut (also known as an open-ended grave) and then started to imagine how my new life would feel if I changed my behaviour.

## The courage to change

**Fear** is always the first emotion we get when we try and learn something new. So, courage is not the absence of fear, but is about feeling the fear and pushing through it and doing it anyway.

Change is like a small death in our minds, we have to grieve the passing of a familiar comfortable way of thinking and doing. We are reluctant to let go of this old familiar behaviour; it is like a physical part of our selves. So, **de-cluttering** our minds of the junk from our past requires courage and is painful but those patterns of behaviour solved a problem in the moment but now they are just out of date and are not delivering the right solutions anymore. It is time for the old patterns to *exit stage left* and let the **new star** behaviour take the stage and show what talents it possesses.

I started to think of the great feeling I have whenever a cheque came in from my self-employed software business. Boy did it feel good, when the project was

44

over and the invoice went in and the client paid, YES! Then I associated that positive feeling with investing my money in property. How good it was going to feel to get a rent cheque every single month for the rest of my life. And not only that, every few years I would could potentially remortgage the property and release some of its equity. Then I would receive an even bigger cheque! By playing this movie in my mind for 30 seconds it helped to create new neural pathways that would fire off the next time I thought about investing. I still felt some fear but it felt less powerful, less controlling of my actions.

**Build those change muscles**

By changing the meaning of what being wealthy means to you, you can start to move towards it, as it is now associated with pleasure and not pain. Like going to the gym; you need to maintain these associations on a regular basis. Continue to visualise *positive* feelings towards getting wealthier and *negative* emotions towards staying where you are right now. Focusing on the **pain** can act as a catalyst towards change. If you really focus on that pain and make it bigger in your mind's eye, it reaches the point where you can't bear it any longer. If you realise that things must change and that only you can change them, then you will be motivated to start changing your old habits.

Tony Robbins also suggests **interrupting** the old unhelpful pattern when it comes up by immediately changing your physical state. So, when you feel yourself thinking negatively about the work required to change, interrupt the thought either with a physical change like standing up suddenly or punching the air, or with a logical question like: What did you have for breakfast this morning? If you interrupt the pattern enough times you will soon find it hard to go back to that old way of thinking.

**A step forwards.**

The combination of meditation to discover my limiting beliefs, and then reassigning those negative beliefs to positive ones, was helping me to think and act differently about wealth. But there were some very deep-seated beliefs buried in my unconscious mind that were still holding me back and so it was time to try a more powerful technique to change these beliefs.

**Hypnotherapy, old school change.**

The German psychologist Sigmund Freud first started his journey into the unconscious mind back in 1885 using hypnosis. This is a technique that induces a state of physical relaxation which allows the mind to focus on suggestions and questions made by a therapist.

Most modern psychotherapy involves *talking* about your feelings and then trying to trace back into your past when these events happened and what decisions you made in that moment about you and the world.

But, if the painful memory or trauma happened before speech developed in your early life, then it's nearly impossible to talk about it. As memory is based on language and so you will not have the language to express it. Instead, you will have more of a *feeling* in your body, like a stomach-ache or feelings of anxiety when you are in certain situations and you won't be able to verbalise to anyone, why you feel that way.

Though many other models of working with the mind have been developed since Freud's time, hypnosis has continued to be used to reveal to the conscious mind that which is buried in the shadows of the unconscious mind. One such modern version of hypnosis is IEMT (Integral Eye Movement Technique).

**Look me in the eye**

As I relaxed in a chair the IEMT hypnotherapist placed a LED light panel in front of me and asked me to follow the horizontally moving LED light with my eyes. Then he asked me to think back to early childhood memories about money. He didn't need to hear the whole story; he just needed one key word to use as a trigger. He asked me to relive the situation in my mind's eye while the light pulsed back and forth from the extreme left to the extreme right of my vision. Then he asked me to rewrite this memory into how I would have liked it to have turned out. While I did this I continued to follow the light source from left to right with my eyes.

The theory behind this approach is it triggers the same neural process as REM (Rapid Eye Movement) sleep. Which is when the mind is writing the events of the day into long-term memory.

This process along, with other techniques for resetting old unhelpful behaviours, are well detailed in the book The Body Keeps the Score by Bessel A. van der Kolk

Even though the technique seemed quite simple and rather odd it did seem to have the effect I wanted; where I had felt pain before about being successful and wealthier I now just felt excited about going on the journey.

With that preliminary work done on re-writing my old unhelpful beliefs, I felt ready to take action and learn the **how-to** of wealth creation.

# Millionaire Mind

*"Rich people play the money game to **WIN**. Poor people play the money game to **NOT** lose"*
– T. Harv Eker

The next book I read on my path to becoming financially free was Secrets of the Millionaire Mind by T. Harv Eker, which enlightened me to a key point that all lottery winners soon discover...

**Your money blueprint.**

We all have a personal money blueprint ingrained in our subconscious minds, and it is this blueprint, more than anything, that will determine our financial lives. You can know everything about your chosen profession, but if your money blueprint is not set for a high level of success, you will never have a lot of money. And if somehow you do, you will most likely lose it!

Most lottery winners, within a few years, end up spending all their winnings and return to the same income they had before winning.

Your financial blueprint consists of a combination of your thoughts, feelings and actions in the area of money.

**Thoughts** lead to feelings.

**Feelings** lead to actions.

**Actions** lead to results.


How did you acquire your money blueprint?

Your money blueprint, was subtly encoded into your unconscious mind first by your parents, and then by your teachers, friends, mentors like physical education coaches, and most powerfully of all, by the old legacy media like newspapers and the BBC.

You may have noticed that the rich guy always ends up being the baddie and usually gets his comeuppance in TV and Hollywood movies. It's all very subtle programming telling you not to even try to be wealthy as other people won't like you and you will probably end up doing something evil!

So, when your subconscious mind needs to choose between the quick memories of deeply rooted beliefs or the slower more effortful route of your rational thoughts, your emotions will always win the race and you will just react instead of truly thinking it through.

## My conditioning to just have a job

I was brought up in a working-class family in Scotland in the 1970s, where having a job was the only way to **make ends meet**. So, when I left home at the age of nineteen, I just went from job to job hoping the next one would pay me more money than the last.

But it didn't matter how much money I earned I always spent it, as that was how I had been programmed by our consumer culture. Those millions of hours of advertising I had consumed through TV, film and billboards had wired my subconscious to buy the latest and greatest gadgets that promised me happiness in exchange for my money. Not only my money, but also my debt, credit cards, personal loans and eventually even mortgages were all ways the capitalist system had normalised my consumption.

My personal money blueprint was set to always being **J**ust **O**ver **B**roke. I could think back to many times in my past when I was flush with extra money and how uncomfortable I was with it. I would usually give it away or buy extravagant presents for others and sometimes even for myself. I would do anything just to get back to my comfort zone of being **J**ust **O**ver **B**roke!

## How the rich and poor think differently

T. Harv Eker presents a list of the many ways that the rich think differently to the poor. As I read through them I reflected on how those beliefs had played out in my life...

1. Rich people believe "I create my life". Poor people believe "Life happens to me".

Yes, I was a victim to life's events and I would blame other things for my misfortune like the economy, the government or my boss. When I blamed others I gave away my power to them, so if I wanted things to improve I had to rely on them changing. Now, that could take a very long time and I was likely to experience a lot of frustration while I waited. But once I took responsibility for my own actions, knowing that the only person I could ever change was myself, that was the day I started creating my own life and my financial freedom.

**2. Rich people play the money game to WIN. Poor people play the money game to NOT lose.**

My unconscious goal in life was just to get by, having just enough to live on. I was totally invested in my delusion that true security was only possible by having a job. When my intention was to have just enough to pay my bills, then unsurprisingly that is exactly how much money I earned and not a penny more. And if I did end up with more than I felt I deserved I spent it or gave it away.

**3. Rich people are committed to being rich. Poor people want to be rich.**

Like most poor people I was carrying negative beliefs about becoming wealthy. Sure, I wanted all the fun that comes with having money, but I believed I would have to work very hard to get it and even worse that no one would like me once I was rich. So, to be truly rich I knew I must commit myself, devote myself unreservedly to the task. No ifs, no buts, no maybes; failure was not an option.

Becoming rich would take hard work but being broke also was hard work. So why not put the hard work into being rich?

## 4. Rich people think big. Poor people think small.

This quote from Marianne Williamson in the book *A Return to Love* says it all for me:

*"Our deepest fear is not that we are inadequate. Our deepest fear is that we are powerful beyond measure. It is our light, not our darkness that most frightens us.*

*We ask ourselves, Who am I to be brilliant, gorgeous, talented, fabulous?*

*Actually, who are you not to be? You are a child of God. Your playing small does not serve the world.*

*There is nothing enlightened about shrinking so that other people won't feel insecure around you. We are all meant to shine, as children do. We were born to make manifest the glory of God that is within us. It's not just in some of us; it's in everyone.*

*And as we let our own light shine, we unconsciously give other people permission to do the same. As we are liberated from our own fear, our presence automatically liberates others."*

**5. Rich people focus on opportunities. Poor people focus on obstacles.**

I discovered a powerful technique in Neuro-Linguistic Programming called reframing.

In reality there is no good or bad, it is just a meaning we choose to give to a situation. This means that I can **choose** to look at the opportunities in a situation, get creative with the limitations presented, and reframe the whole event as one that is useful to me. I now grow the most when I'm at the edge of my comfort zone and the least when I play it safe.

T. Harv Eker goes on to say a key point about building wealth:

*"If you want to get rich, focus on **making**, **keeping** and **investing** your money. If you want to be poor, focus on **spending** your money. Remember what you focus on expands."*

6. Rich people admire other rich and successful people. Poor people resent rich and successful people.

With my working-class upbringing I definitely disliked rich people but, to my surprise, the more wealthy, self-made rich people I met, the more I realised what expansive thinkers they were; the art of the possible was their mantra and with the money they had created they were able to help others.

This is exemplified by Bill Gates who has committed to give away the vast majority of his fortune and the fortunes of many of the richest people in the world.

As Harv says: *"Bless that which you want."*

Next time you see a rich person in an expensive car or house then bless that person, because if you resent what people have then how can you ever have it too?

**7. Rich people associate with positive, successful people. Poor people associate with negative or unsuccessful people.**

Successful people look at other successful people as models to learn from. "If they can do it so can I". I have a friend who has built a property portfolio of around 20 properties all by himself, he has a real **can do** attitude and so it was to him that I turned for guidance and inspiration when I was ready to buy my first rental property.

Whilst my friends with day jobs were telling me how risky it all was, I for once, was smart enough to listen to the guy who had already done it and not to the **play it safe** brigade. And 5 years later I was financially free, and my friends with their day jobs, still had their day jobs!

**8. Rich people are willing to promote themselves and their value. Poor people think negatively about selling and promotion.**

No matter what you do in life, at some point you do have to sell yourself, be it at a job interview or to a potential romantic partner you spot in a bar. To learn how to sell yourself, a great book to start with is *How to sell anything to anyone* by Jo Owen. As Harv says: "Rich people are usually leaders and all great leaders are great promoters. To be a leader, you must inherently have followers and supporters, which means that you have to be adept at selling, inspiring and motivating people to buy your vision. Leaders earn a lot more than followers!"

**9. Rich people are bigger than their problems. Poor people are smaller than their problems.**

Harv states: "The size of the problem is never the issue, what matters is the size of you. So, you need to grow yourself so that you are bigger than any problem."

When I started off building my property portfolio I was hit with a massive problem. Where was I going to get the money from? I asked my highly successful friend who had bought over 20 properties in 15 years and he said: "There is money everywhere; you just have to find people who have it but don't have the time to use it!" So, I started to ask around my network of friends and their friends and within a few short weeks I had raised over £300,000!

**10. Rich people are excellent receivers. Poor people are poor receivers.**

My low self-esteem had caused me to have a strong poverty mentality. I had always been a giver and not a receiver in my life. These were deep-seated beliefs and so I needed the help of a Life Coach to work through my conditioning. When I started believing I was worthy of being rich I started to receive the help and money that I needed to create wealth for myself. The fear that becoming rich would turn me into the stereotypical mean Scrooge character was summed up well by Harv when he said "Money will only make you more of what you already are." So, if you are a generous person then having more money will allow you to be even more generous!

## 11. Rich people choose to get paid based on results. Poor people choose to get paid based on time.

I had spent 20 years being paid by the hour as a software developer. During this time, I knew that my wealth was limited to the number of hours in a day and how valuable my knowledge was. After reading Harv's book I started to offer clients the option of paying me less per hour but also sharing in the profit of the enterprise. I was now even more committed to the success of the project than before, when I just picked up my pay cheque at the end of the job.

## 12. Rich people think "both". Poor people think "either/or".

My thinking used to be that you are either poor and happy or rich and friendless! But what I discovered was that I could have both money and friends; I could focus on my business needs and still go out and play. Being financially free is ultimately about having a balance in your life between working to create wealth and playing to enjoy it.

## 13. Rich people focus on their net worth. Poor people focus on their working income.

As Harv says: "The true measure of wealth is net worth, not working income." So, I worked out how much money I would have if I liquidated every asset I owned and realised that I had a long way to go to become a Net Millionaire.

Harv also encourages reducing your expenses

each month to increase your income. What if I sold or rented out my home and moved in with a friend and then took those savings and invested them? I could be several hundred pounds a month better off; compounded over the next 20 years, until I retire, that is over £100,000!

**14. Rich people manage their money well. Poor people mismanage their money well.**

Harv makes the point that if you wait until you are rich before learning how to manage your money then you will never be rich. Either you control your money, or it will control you! Harv recommends putting 10% away for long term savings, 10% for play, 10% for investing in assets or businesses that provide passive income, 10% for your continued education and 10% to give away to worthy causes. The remaining 50% is to live on. By dividing your income in this way, you can start taking **responsibility** for your financial freedom.

## 15. Rich people have their money work hard for them. Poor people work hard for their money.

Harv points out that you do have to work hard for your money. But for rich people this is a temporary situation. For poor people, it's permanent. Rich people understand that **you** have to work hard until your **money** works hard enough to take your place. The rich understand that the more your money works for you, the less you will have to work for it.

And I can report this view to be true. Since I discovered the concept of *passive income* and put my money to work for me I now work when I want to while my money always works 24/7 for me!

## 16. Rich people act in spite of fear. Poor people let fear stop them.

Courage is not the absence of fear but feeling the fear and doing it anyway. Research has shown that the fear of losing money is more powerful than the desire to have more money. And so, we stay stuck in fear and poverty.

As Harv says: "If you are willing to do only what's easy, life will be hard. But if you are willing to do what's hard, life will be easy."

**17. Rich people constantly learn and grow. Poor people think they already know.**

I know what I know and I have a sense of what I don't know **but** far larger is what I don't know I don't know! So, every time I met a person who knew more about making money than me I asked them to tell me how they did it. I read as many books on money, investing, trading and property developing that I could find. And fifteen years on into this journey I still feel I have a lot to learn. You can be right or you can be rich, but you can't be both.

**Time to take action**

I was starting to realise that becoming financially free was going to take a lot harder work and involve a lot more changing of my beliefs, than I had first thought.

There were a lot of ingrained limiting beliefs in me about wealth and so I knew I was going to need help to break through them and finally take action. I needed someone who had already been there, done it and learned the hard lessons of becoming financially free...

## Your network

*"The richest people in the world build networks. Everyone else looks for work." – Robert Kiyosaki*

After reading Robert Kiyosaki's book _Rich Dad Poor Dad_ I realised I needed to acquire some high net worth assets that would pay me a passive income. As Kiyosaki points out, one of the best ways of generating passive income is to buy property and rent it out. It was 2006 and all around me property was racing up in value in the UK by more than 10% a year, including my own home.

### Every master starts out as a disaster

My first faltering step to acquiring some assets was to check out a **new build** development happening right on my doorstep in Brighton. The glossy brochure for the soon to be completed 100 flats talked excitedly about how great the demand would be for these modern flats situated right next to the train station in Brighton. It seemed such an easy option; I didn't have to spend huge amounts of my precious time dealing with estate agents and even more time dealing with builders to renovate the place. I could just buy a brand new shiny flat from the lovely sales person next to me who was offering me free coffee along with my glossy brochure!

When I got home I excitedly rang my property developer friend JC and told him

*"It's going to be so easy; I can buy a brand new two-bedroom apartment for a mere £250,000 and earn a rental return of £800 a month!"*

He stopped me right there and calmly pointed out that I should never buy new build, especially not in a large block of flats, as that meant I was competing against many other new landlords all trying to rent out their properties at the same time and it would be a race to the bottom to offer the cheapest rents. On top of that every 10 years or so there would be a massive maintenance bill to scaffold the entire block to repair the brickwork and the roof, wiping out any profits made from the rents.

## Finding my guru

I knew then in JC I had found the ally I needed to learn how to build up my property portfolio. It is one of those universal truths that when we start to get clear on what we want in life we then meet the right people to help us get it. I had known JC for about 6 years and knew he had been building a property portfolio of his own for about fifteen years, but I had never made the connection until then that he could help me. This is the power of educating yourself about how the rich think. They don't see *limitations*; they see **opportunities** and they use the people they know to help them; they are not afraid to ask for help in achieving something beyond their current capabilities.

I was starting to see through the delusion of **doing it all by myself**. The true way to prosperity was building a network of people that could help me, people who had specific skills or money that they would share with me to help me generate wealth for both them and me.

**Think Win-Win**

As Steven Covey points out in his book – *The 7 habits of highly effective people* – create relationships with people where you both win and get something out of the deal. So often we have a **Job Mentality,** which teaches us that our boss is the enemy and we must do everything we can to get the most money, holidays and perks out of them. A **win** for all is ultimately a better long-term solution than if only one person in a situation gets their way.

**Friends are the new bank**

It is always far easier to negotiate terms with friends or their friends than it is with a bank. Banks have lost the personal touch; it all comes down to computer algorithms with their binary logic decreeing whether you are a good risk or not; and as the financial crash of 2008 had shown us all, those algorithms were just plain dangerous.

I found negotiating with people much easier than trying to persuade a computer algorithm that my plans were a good investment.

In the end I paid just £10 for a basic legal document called a **Promissory Note** from the website lawdepot.co.uk and with that I was able to borrow over

**£300,000** from friends and provide them with a legal proof of the loan.

And I used that borrowed money from friends along with a mortgage from a bank to help buy a house that I converted into 3 flats (See Chapter 7).

## Online networks of entrepreneurial talent

The Internet has allowed us all to extend our personal networks beyond the limits of our social and business contacts. To help me with day-to-day issues around buying property I used several property forums like PropertyTribes.com where fellow UK property developers, with varying ranges of experience, were happy to share their knowledge with me for free. This is the great gift of the information age we now live in; the ability to connect with experts from around the world who happily share their hard-won knowledge with us, often for free.

Finding the right people to work with can be hard if you have no experience in the ways of creating wealth independently. Often you need access to people with skills that are not available in your own personal network. A good place to start finding connections is LinkedIn.com

## Time to take action

By now I had re-educated myself about the power of owning assets that would generate a passive income for me for the rest of my life. I had made some great contacts through friends and had access to several online resources where I could get good help and support.

So now it was time to put all of that knowledge into practice and take action. Taking action is the bridge between your inner mindset and the outer world.

But I felt some resistance to taking action. Why was that. Was it my fear of failure? Fear of it not being the absolutely perfect time to buy property or the fear of taking a risk with all that money?

The fear of "what if..." kept coming up and I knew I needed courage to take the first step. I had learned that courage is not the absence of fear but feeling the fear and doing it anyway. Having a great idea does not generate success. In fact, putting into action an average idea is far better than holding onto that perfect plan and waiting for the perfect conditions before taking action.

While searching for inspiration on the internet I found this quote by a mountaineer planning to climb Everest:

*Until one is committed, there is hesitancy, the chance to draw back. Concerning all acts of initiative (and creation), there is one elementary truth that ignorance of which kills countless ideas and splendid plans: that the moment one definitely commits oneself, then Providence moves too. All sorts of things occur to help one that would never otherwise have occurred.*

*A whole stream of events issues from the decision, raising in one's favour all manner of unforeseen incidents and meetings and material assistance, which no man could have dreamed would have come his way.*

*Whatever you can do, or dream you can do, begin it. Boldness has genius, power, and magic in it. Begin it now.*

Scottish mountaineer William Hutchinson Murray, 1951 (from the original by Goethe).

Being lucky to have a friend, JC, who was an expert in buying and renting out property, I decided to commit and see what providence delivered with his guidance.

## Passive Income ideas

Buying and renting out property is not the only way to creative passive income for yourself. You may not have the capital required to buy property, so let's look at a few other options.

**1. Selling other people's products** – you don't have to come up with a brand-new product or service; you can simply sell other people's innovative products. The most famous version of that is Fulfilled by Amazon where you source products and then Amazon stores them and ships them to your customers.

**2. Owning licenses for intellectual products** – creating a book, music, photographs, videos or artwork. These can all be sold or licensed to other people. Services like Amazon and Spotify can help you to do this with no upfront costs.

**3. Owning land** – you don't need to go through all the hassle of building a property and renting it out. You can instead just own the land that a building is sitting on and receive a rent from the owner every year. Owning car parking spaces are another low-cost and low-maintenance way of generating cash flow.

**4. Buying hotel rooms** – this can be a really simple way of earning passive income without having to even worry about finding a property and renting it out. All of the main hotel chains offer this service. A great article on the *Property Investor* site provides more information about this.

**5. Trading currencies and commodities on the foreign exchange markets (Forex).** I talk about my experience of this in Chapter 8. Forex is not strictly a passive income approach, it requires daily attention and caries a lot of risk, but if you have the right mindset for trading it can be very lucrative and it is tax free in the UK.

**6. Tax Liens** – In the USA when property owners get into arrears with their property taxes the local state takes ownership of the property. Then investors like you and I can take on the risk of paying those taxes and receive a high interest rate (18%+) on the debt until it's paid off by the owner. And if the owner does not pay it off you get to keep the property for free! Find out more at the US Tax Lien Association.

**7. Your life experiences** – think about all of your life experiences and then ask yourself: *Would someone find my knowledge valuable?* You could then write a book about your experiences (just like I have done), or run a one-day course on the subject. You could also create a blog and start building a following which generates income from affiliate links, just as Pat Linn did at SmartPassiveIncome.com.

These are just a few ideas to get you started. Google or Bing are your friends, so just type in your idea and see what the World Wide Web thinks about it; chances are someone else has already started it which is a sign there is a business there!

# PART 2

~

## Doing

*"How you do anything, is how you do everything."* - **T. Harv Eker**

# Rules for buying property

*"Ninety percent of all millionaires become so through owning real estate" – Andrew Carnegie*

If you ask any wealthy person where they have their money invested, most will say property. It's how the rich have built and, more importantly, held onto their wealth through the generations. So, I knew that property had to be one of the pillars of wealth in my new financially freedom blueprint.

It's relatively easy to buy a property; the hard bit is buying one that makes you money from day one. Below are some of the rules I learned on my journey to buying and owning investment properties.

## Rule 1 – Profit starts with what you pay for it

The main factor determining whether your investment will be profitable is **how much you pay for it in the first place**! No matter how much potential for growth the estate agent tells you it has, if the price is too high, it will take you many extra years to move into profit. You wouldn't open a savings account that lost you money for the first few years, so why do that with a property? If the price is too high to make a profit from renting it out then walk away, a better property will come along eventually.

## Rule 2 – Off plan is off limits

Don't buy off-plan; it may take another 1-2 years before it's finished by which time the property market may have changed dramatically. With any newly built property you are going to be paying top price for it as the property developer needs to make back all his costs for building it. This consideration disappears after a building is many years old

## Rule 3 – Buy rundown over high finish

Don't buy a property that is finished to a high standard; you are going to be paying for all that glitz. It is much better to buy a slightly rundown property and then spend a small amount renovating it. It will cost you or your builder much less to do the work as you can control what work is done.

Remember, most renters want a **good finish** not an expensive finish and most rental properties need redecorating every 5 years due to the wear and tear of tenants living in them. So, it is not worth putting in a real marble kitchen top, you are better off with an imitation one as in five years' time it probably won't be in fashion anymore.

## Rule 4 – A house is better than a flat

Don't buy a flat in a block, because about every 10 years they are going to have to put scaffolding up to maintain the building and that costs a lot of money. That could make the difference between a profitable long term asset and a losing one. Plus you don't want to be competing with other landlords in the same block marketing exactly the same kind of flat as yours. That then becomes a race to the bottom to offer the lowest rent. Furthermore, with a house you can add value to the property by building an extension or a loft conversion, adding extra rooms and thereby increasing your rental income.

## Rule 5 – Befriend your estate agent

Let the estate agent know you're open to buying difficult properties; ones they can't shift or ones where they need to sell very quickly. People in a hurry are much more open to negotiating on price than people who are just testing the market to see how much they can get. So, build up a good relationship with your local estate agents, be polite to them and always follow through with promises you make; if a property is not for you say so clearly to save them wasting their time chasing you.

## Rule 6 – Don't buy in an up-and-coming area

Buy a property in a good area for rentals. Don't buy in an up-and-coming area; it can take decades for an area **to arrive.** Buy the best property you can afford in an area that is already thriving. That way when the next down-turn comes along your property will weather the storm and come out the other side quicker and worth more than properties bought in the new-builds in the up-and-coming areas!

## Rule 7 – Be interested in your own wealth

No one is as interested in your wealth as much as you are. In other words, check everything, all of the documents from your solicitor and estate agent, and when you come to rent out the property double check all the references you receive from the tenants. Yes, the letting agent **should** have done that but they get paid for finding you tenants not whether they still pay the rent 6 months down the line.

It is worth running your own property lets, most agents pay very little attention to your property; you are just one of hundreds they are looking after. That leaky radiator they take a month to fix can do huge damage to your wooden floors and the ceiling beneath it.

### Rule 8 – Learn how to write your own contracts

Learn how to write your own contracts. I chose to learn about how to write contracts after my solicitor wanted to charge me £500 to draw up a very simple contract. First I discovered www.lawdepot.co.uk and paid just £10 for a simple contract. Then I read up on a few legal websites about the basic rules of a contract and that helped
me modify the contract to exactly fit my needs. I have reused that same contract 6 times to help me borrow over £300,000.

### Rule 9 – Inflation is your friend

I did worry about borrowing a large sum of money as one day the mortgage term would expire and the bank would want its money back, right?. But when I would meet people who had bought their homes more than 25 years ago, the thing that struck me most was how small the original sum borrowed now appeared, it was usually in the region of just a few thousand pounds.

So many people don't buy property because they are afraid of being in debt. Though technically a mortgage is a *security* and not a debt, as it is secured against a physical asset.

But the money you borrow for your rental property today will effectively become **frozen in time.** Thanks to inflation, that £200,000 you borrowed from the mortgage company will appear quite paltry in 25 years from now. And the fact the property is still being rented out and making a profit will mean that most mortgage companies will be happy to lend to you again and again no matter how old you are. **A rental property is a business** after all, not your own home, so banks will look at the business case first and not your age as they would with a mortgage on your own home.

**Note:** Mortgage lending rules change all the time, so you do need to keep an eye on the rules. But the basic business case normally shines through despite the destructive government interference in the free market.

### Rule 10 – It's not a get rich quick scheme

There are a lot of setup costs with buying a rental property. The government want their property tax, the solicitor wants paying for handling the deal, the mortgage company wants a fee to lend to you and the builder wants paying for renovating your property. So, you are going to be spending a lot of money upfront as well as probably paying the full market value for the property. Property is not a get-rich-quick scheme; it is a **get rich, very slowly scheme,** which is probably going to take about 5 years to start making a decent profit, and then another 10 years before you get back your initial investment. So, you are going to have to be patient. But all good investments take time to mature. Avoid any investment that promises more than 10% return in a year. If it sounds too good to be true, then it normally is!

The devil is in the detail, so in the next chapter I am going to describe my experience of buying my first rental property.

# My first rental property

## Use other people's money

With these rules from the previous chapter now embedded in me I put the first rule of the rich into play: using **other people's money**.

My main opportunity to access *other people's money* was from my own home by **releasing equity**. Equity is just a posh word for an asset you have a stake in, hence the stock market is referred to as the equity markets by finance folks, as you own a part of each company you have bought shares in.

I released equity by simply getting a new mortgage on my home for a higher amount than my current mortgage of £50,000. This released or *leveraged* £150,000 of my property's value (equity), as cash that I could spend. This is a very powerful mechanism; transferring partial ownership of an asset to a bank, in exchange for money. It was also a validation of the idea that property is a good investment when a bank is willing to lend 85% of its value to you. I thought this was an incredible mechanism; being able to get the cash value of my own home but yet still being able to make use of the asset by living in it.

## A distressed seller

Next, I had to find a property that was going to make me money from day one. Luckily my friend JC was well connected with the local estate agents in London and one morning in early August 2006 he received a phone call from an agent that had just had a sale drop through that morning; the vendor was desperate to get shot of the house as she now lived on the other side of the world and it was just too much hassle to keep renting it out. Perfect. A seller in a hurry is always a good person to negotiate with because:

*"a person who needs it the most, is always in the weakest position."*

When JC looked round the 3-bedroom house it was a bit of a mess inside as students were living in it; there were mattresses on the floor and sarongs hanging in the window for curtains, but the building was sound. It was the perfect deal as normal buyers were rejecting it because of these superficial issues. I agreed to the newly reduced asking price and the deal was agreed that same day for £250,000.

Update: In 2023 this house is now worth £650,000!

## The power of levers

In 2006 Buy-to-let mortgages only required a 15% deposit and the bank would lend you the other 85%. This was a new concept to me, **leveraging** a small amount of money into a larger sum of money. I put down a deposit of £37,500 and the bank invested the rest, £212,500. This is the power of leveraging *other people's money.*

So, as the property went up in value by roughly 10% a year, I was not just getting a simple 10% increase on my £37,500 (£3,750) but additionally on the bank's money too. Therefore, 10% of £250,000 equalled £25,000 a year!

As Archimedes discovered, a small amount of effort on one side of a lever generates a larger amount of lift on the other side, and the same is true with money!

### Renovating
The next job was to bring the property up to a **good enough standard,** so as to be attractive to young

professional renters. I spent about £20,000 doing modest renovations to the property – a new bathroom suite, tiling the kitchen, repainting the existing kitchen cupboards, painting the inside of the house and adding new carpets; this was all done in 8 weeks.

**Note:** It's key to not overdo the decoration for a rental property. Most tenants are happy with a clean and freshly decorated property. People are very price sensitive when they rent, so paying extra for a high-end finish is not on the agenda for the average renter.

### Property for free

I had bought the property below market value, due to the owner being in a hurry to sell, and I had renovated the building to a good standard. Now it was time to release some of that newly created value by asking the mortgage company for a *Further Advance.*

The mortgage company surveyor gave the property a new value of £350,000. So, in just 3 months I had made £100,000!

In total I got back £83,000 from the mortgage company, which paid back all the money I had invested into the property plus an extra £10,000 of cash just for me. And, it rented out very easily and was making me a profit of £200 a month!

Effectively I had bought the property for nothing, not a single penny of my money was now in that asset, and it had paid me a bonus of £10,000 and was generating £2,400 a year rental profit. I definitely wanted to do another one of these, as quickly as possible!

Update: in 2023 it makes £16,800 a year profit

My first rental property
Archway, North London, UK

# Build your own.

*"If you build it, they will come"*
*The movie 'Field of Dreams'*

It was now the middle of 2007 and the property market was at its peak in London, property was going so quickly that one hardly had a chance to see a property before it was sold, usually for more than the asking price.

Markets in any asset class go through periods when the price becomes too high and at times like these you need to work around the problem and look for different ways to acquiring valuable assets.

The answer to high house prices was a bold and simple one. I would have to build my own apartments; it was the only affordable way to do it. But to buy a house in North London and convert it into say, 3 apartments, would take around £500,000, and that was five times more than I had.

## Finding a business partner

We would need around £350,000 to do a development, to put down a 25% deposit of £212,000, and pay stamp duty of 4% totalling £34,000. So, in total I needed £596,000. At most I had £150,000 to invest, so where would I raise the rest? I looked into development finance but the fees and interest rates of 20% made the deal unprofitable, and profit was why I was doing it in the first place, not the joy of talking to the planning department for the next year. Then JC stepped in and firstly put me in touch with a friend of his, ES, who had been thinking about investing in property for a while but hadn't taken the plunge yet. So, we both met around his kitchen table drinking herbal tea and there and the chose to form a partnership that was to last the next 20 years.

I had learned from my mistakes in the past when working with friends; although it is great to trust people, it is always best to get your *agreement in writing* as it is amazing how quickly people forget what they agreed to.

We had a solicitor draw up a **Joint Venture Agreement** which outlines who is responsible for what. We agreed that I would deal with all the administration and financial stuff and that ES would be onsite checking that the building work was running to schedule.

## Finding investors

They say it is "who you know in this world" that counts and I was about to learn just how true that was.

Even though ES and I were combining our money we still needed to find the estimated development costs of £350,000.

Our property guru JC stepped in again and introduced us to a friend of his who wanted to invest in property but did not have the time to do it. We agreed a loan of £100,000 at 12% interest payable at the end of the year.

Note: The Bank of England interest rate was at 5.75% in 2007, so this was a very reasonable rate to pay considering the risk involved.

The legal framework for the loan was based on a £10 *promissory note* I downloaded from the lawdepot.co.uk website; you don't have to spend hundreds of pounds on bespoke legal documents.

As a result of borrowing money this way, I saved on the usual 1%-2% arrangement fees that are charged for development finance as well as paying a much-reduced interest rate of 12%, compared with the 20+% that a commercia loan could charge. It's by paying attention to these details on a big development project that can make the difference between profit or loss.

Next, through a mix of going to networking events and putting the call out to friends, I found two people with £100,000 each to invest, and used the same *promissory note* as before.

This decision to use ordinary people instead of banks would prove crucial to weathering the storm of the 2008/9 banking crisis that lay ahead of us, as people are always easier to negotiate with than faceless banks.

**Let the work commence**

In early 2008 we completed the purchase and the conversion work began a few weeks later. It took over 10 months to do the conversion work as we had numerous setbacks, with the construction and even the council withdrawing our planning permission. But when you fully *commit* to a project these issues just become bumps in the road, not a reason to give up. And when you do overcome them it feels like a real *punch in the air* victory.

## Lessons learned

So here are the keys points we learned during the development that will hopefully help you in your adventures into property development.

1. The devil is in the detail, so check everything and assume nothing. If you break the word assume down it makes an "**ass** of **u** and **me**"!

2. When people say "No, it can't be done", don't believe them and find a way that it can.

3. When dealing with your local council's planning department check and chase every detail, they are just not motivated to help you. So, you need to become an expert at their job.

4. You are responsible for every detail, not the builder, architect or the council.

5. Choose your team with discernment. Business partners can just as easily turn into enemies as they can friends.

6. Build a team. Everyone can be part of your success team, the mortgage broker, the investor and the key

cutter. If you involve them in the project then support can arrive in the most unusual but often perfect ways.

7. You get out what you put in. If you're after good yields on your investment, invest a little more on the fixtures and fittings, not only will they last a little longer, your tenants will recognise quality and treat the property with more respect!

8. Take your time creating a comprehensive contract between the builder and yourself, with a clear payment schedule based on the progress stages of the project.

9. Check that the builder is insured. We had a wall fall down on one of the builders when the site manager was absent and if he had been seriously hurt then he could have sued us!

10. Find a mentor; the road can be plagued with pot holes and having a guide helps you to sleep at night.

11. Don't ever give up, even if the planning department say that your entire development is illegal!

The Finished Property - Tufnell Park, London, UK

## The lure of the silver screen

*"Hollywood is a place where they'll pay you a thousand dollars for a kiss and fifty cents for your soul."*
Marilyn Monroe

One of the key lessons you learn when investing your money is that every asset class, like property, stocks, crypto, bonds, gold etc all have their season.

First its spring, that's when the early adopter's step in and get excited about the opportunity and truly do make the 10x times returns. But your average person won't be aware of these yet, you have to be on the inside to know. This is the world of Angel Investors and Venture Capital, incredibly high risk investing as most of these opportunities will fail once winter comes. But, the smart people get out before then leaving the late comers to absorb the loses.

Next it's summer time and this is when everybody wakes up to the opportunity. You start reading articles in the press and it comes up in conversation in the pub or dinner parties. And then people start pilling in and the asset price starts to climb exponentially.

But inevitably winter comes and the fall begins. That once blooming verdant asset now feels like a useless husk. You have two choices here, weather the season and wait for spring again or sell up, get what you can for what remains and store those remaining funds away until spring.

By 2012 I felt that I was in the depths of winter, the recession was in full swing and the ease of borrowing and investing in property had withered on the vine. I was ready to get out of my property investment but my business partner ES didn't want to sell. So, I had to look around for a different asset class, something a little bit more dynamic than property.

## The great British film industry

As a kid I had escaped to my local cinema in Irvine to lose myself in the great movies of the 1970s and 1980s like Star Wars, Indiana Jones and Gregory's Girl.

Now, Gregory's Girl was shot in a housing scheme near where I lived, and its tale of ordinary folk first planted the seed that it was possible for someone like me to make a movie.

With the financial freedom I had gained from my property investments I decided to attend my local film school in Brighton where I learned about story structure, film editing and how to produce a movie.

I was also volunteering at a small local theatre in Brighton, which was run mainly by volunteers with the occasional professional actor hired in for their monthly plays.

It was here that I met aspiring film director James Newton. He had had some early experience acting in a TV soap but really wanted to Direct.

At first we made a few short films and even took one to the Cannes film festival, where we quickly realised no one wanted to buy short films.

So, we agreed that surely making a full-length feature film couldn't be much more work than making a short film.

How very naive and wrong we were!

## How to make a movie on a micro-budget

Most low-budget movies are made for at least a few million pounds but we felt confident that we could make ours for less than half a million pounds. Which is the cost of the catering budget on most movie sets.

James wanted to recreate the movies of his childhood, where a bunch of kids go on adventure, have fun, get into trouble but ultimately learn something about themselves and friendship. This would be a live action kids' film, to get away from the endless animated content that was dominating the kids film market at the time.

I was given the glamourous title of **Executive Producer,** which really just meant, I had to find the money.

I knew the project was risky, so I applied a golden rule of thumb in investing circles, to not put all my eggs in one basket and so I choose to only risk 10% of my available capital into this risky enterprise.

Unlike my previous investment in property, which had a physical asset to sell at the end of it. A movie was a more intangible type of asset to invest in.

Because a film is just an idea, with some words on a page. Then you have to find some actors to agree to be in the film, which is a bit like herding cats, as one actor states they will only be in it, if a more important actor is in it too. And then the more important actor only has a 2-week window free the next year to do it. And often a better offer comes along just as you were about to start filming and then the whole house of cards collapses.

As the rest of the team were trying to finalise the script and hire decent actors, I was still struggling to find investors. Then on one fateful day, whilst visiting the Director, he received a call that one of the other investors to be told he was pulling out his money, even though filming was due to start in a few months' time.

As I listened to this news, instead of taking the setback calmly, the little kid in me that so wanted to make a film, to have his name up in lights, to be remembered for creating a work of art, spoke up and I found myself offering to replace the lost investment!

So, now I was committed to putting 70% of my available capital into a very risky investment. I tried to back out of it later but partly embarrassment on my part and refusal by the director to give the money back meant I was fully committed.

I rationalised my mistake by believing even more in the group delusion that we were maverick film makers and were going to make yet another classic British movie that would win awards and be fondly remembered by generations of families and kids.

Over the next two years our film 2:Hrs was eventually cast, shot and edited with endless setbacks and disagreements between us all. It was like being in a slow-motion trainwreck as the reality of making something as complex as a movie by a team of people who really had no idea how to do it. In particular the other producers showed an alarming level of incompetence and reminded me yet again that I must do my due diligence on the people I get into business with.

### Roll-out the red carpet

But then one day, after all the heartache, the film was finally finished and we had our world premiere at the Rio Cinema in London on January 2018 with the cast and crew in attendance. I remember sitting there and thinking that is either the worst film I have ever watched or I was just too old to enjoy a kid's film now.

They say in the movie business there are only 2 kinds of films, the great movies and all the rest. It was clear to me we had definitely made a movie that was going to join the latter category.

But *hope springs eternal* and so we still had to try and sell this clunky movie to a film distributor under the faint hope we investors could get our money back.

We again underestimated how tough that would be too. Cinemas don't just put anybody's film on their screens, they have contracts with large distributors that have been establish for decades.

As a small independent film maker, you are effectively just a Mino floundering in the vast sea that is the film distribution business. The distributor is a shark that can smell blood in the water and they size you up and sign you up to a contract where they keep most of the profit while you pay for their marketing costs and trips to film festivals to promote your film.

We sold the film to numerous countries around the world but to date it has brought in no more than a few thousand pounds of profit to us. At this rate it will take to the end of the century to pay us back.

**Slow and steady wins the race**

The key lesson I learned is that often times, slow, boring investments like property will actually make you wealthier over the long term (10-20 years) than that new exciting opportunity you just saw a video about on social media.

*If it sounds too good to be true, then it is!*

## A new direction

I really should have taken some *independent financial advice* before committing so much money to such a risky investment. But no experience is ever a wasted one, there is always new information in the unknown, which is why we are drawn to explore it.

While trying to persuade people to invest in the 2:Hrs movie, one potential investor turned asked,

"Don't you have to be an authorised *Financial Advisor* to be asking people for an investment into a movie?"

In truth I didn't know what a Financial Advisor was or did. So, next day I called one up and we chatted through how the UK investment world worked and even though I could ask people for money without being one, I felt it would help my chances if I could quickly train as one.

The financial advisor on the phone said, "It's easy to start training as Financial Advisor, the exams are modular and available online and you can do them in your own time. Once you have passed all six of them you can call yourself a Financial Advisor."

Great I thought, I'm sure I can complete them within a year, one exam every 2 months and then I would be free to ask people to invest in my movie!

After a whole year I had passed five of the exams but the final exam of the six was the hardest and I missed the pass mark by 7 points! But not deterred I started applying for jobs as a financial adviser hoping I could gain some job experience that would help me pass this last exam. I was now aged 53 and no one wanted to hire an old guy like me, despite my grey-hairs and wrinkles being an asset in that world.

One potential employer told me straight, he said look, you have no experience in financial services, so unlikely that anyone will employ you. Your best bet is to start at the bottom and become a mortgage broker, once you've done that for six months, then come back and see me.

So, I called up my own mortgage broker Simon, to ask his advice on how to get a job in his industry and he said, "Come and work for me!" and so I did, just as the 2020 global Covid pandemic began and everyone was being forced to work from home.

I ended up working as a mortgage broker for the next two-and-a-half years but I used that time to study hard as well and eventually passed my final exam on the third attempt. I was now a qualified Financial Adviser five years after I started the journey.

After a brief stint working for a large financial advisory firm in 2022, I decided that world wasn't for me, just way too many rules for such a rebel as me. I wanted the freedom to educate people about money without having to worry about selling them a pension or an insurance policy.

## Teach a person how to fish

So, after nearly two decades of educating myself, taking action and making lots of mistakes I finally felt it was time to give back.

Over that time, I have meet hundreds of people whose real problem was just not understanding their financial world.

Poor investment decisions, be it choosing not to save or to invest into the wrong kind of assets, like cryptocurrencies, was costing them their futures.

I now offer people who want to learn a series of financial coaching sessions to help them understand why they do what they do and then support them to change that behaviour.

For more information check out my website below.

www.KevinHBoyd.com

# PART 3

~

## Being

*"Your True Self is your unconditioned self,
free from craving and attachment"*

*The Buddha*

# The New Rich

*"Everything popular is wrong" – Tim Ferriss*

Now I was financially free – I was receiving enough money from my four rental units to cover my mortgage, utility bills and food, plus a bit extra for socialising. At last, I could stop worrying about money and just hang-out, do what I wanted each day, read all those books I've been meaning to read, write a book even!

## Seven-day weekend

But after a while I hit an existential problem – what was I actually going to do with my seven-day weekend? As the months rolled by I became increasingly aware that taking away the daily struggle to pay the bills had left me with a lack of purpose in my life. Since I had entered the world of work at the age of nineteen I had been focused on this one goal, to stop having to go to work each day because I thought, then I would be truly free and could do whatever I wanted!

But I had been working for nearly 30 years by now, all I knew was how to get up each day and go to work. As each day ticked by I felt increasingly directionless and unfulfilled. I felt no urgency to get out of bed and get on with my day, as the bills would still be paid even if I just watched TV all day for the rest of my life!

**The New Rich**

Then, by the joys of Amazon's *Customers Who Bought This Item Also Bought This,* I discovered the book *The 4-hour work week* by Tim Ferriss.

Tim Ferris defines a new social class, **The New Rich.**

These are people who have freed themselves from the everyday Faustian contract of exchanging their time for money. They generate all of their income passively or with minimal input each day, this is often achieved by outsourcing a lot of their work to Virtual Personal Assistants who often work in developing countries and charge a fraction of what it costs in the West.

The New Rich also challenge the rules; they find smarter ways to work than turning up to the office for 8 hours a day, 5 days a week. With the advent of mobile technologies like Zoom and iPhones your office can be anywhere in the world, including the beach! Your boss probably doesn't care where you are as long as you deliver good work and often working away from the office is far more productive. I had been working remotely via the Internet since the late 1990s and often found that I was further ahead in my work than my colleagues who were stuck back in the office; I had also avoided the daily grind of the commute into work which reduced my stress levels and saved me money and gave me a more positive outlook on the work I was doing.

Traditional retirement is a flawed idea, as it is predicated on the assumption that you dislike your job and want to stop doing it when you are age 67. Most people won't be able to retire and maintain their standard of living due to inflation reducing their savings or pension pot by 2% to 10% a year. And if you do love your job then when you do retire you'll go crazy with the lack of things to do!

The New Rich instead plan to spread many **mini-retirements** throughout their lives instead of saving it all up for the end of life.

The New Rich don't necessarily have lots of money but what they do have is lots of **free time** and they spend that free time the way they want to by having great experiences like travelling, volunteering or learning new skills.

I know I get bored pretty easily, so it makes sense to fill my life with a balance of play and work. But work I'm passionate about, that I can build into a business, and when I've had enough fun with that business, I am free to move onto the next thing that interest me because I have the financial freedom to do so.

The thought of just doing one or two jobs or careers, that I don't enjoy, just for the money and then retiring and sitting around doing nothing of meaning all day actually fills me with horror!

And in truth we are all living much longer and our governments can't afford to have us all sitting around for nearly thirty years being economically inactive whilst taking state benefits. We need to create a new way of living that allows people to be productive and happy their whole lives.

This reframing of the situation I found myself in was empowering. I remembered that 30 years ago when backpacking around the world I found myself in some of the top surfing spots in the world like Hawaii, Bali and Bondi beach in Australia. As I sat there on Bondi beach, watching these guys dance in and out of the waves on their surfboards, I made a promise to myself that one day I would return and join them in the surf.

## Time to hit the gym

I realised that if I didn't take the opportunity right now to learn to surf at the age of 45 there was no way I would be able to do it when I **retired** at 67. But would I even be able to do it now? Like most middle-aged people I only went to the gym every now and then – just to justify the monthly membership fee; my stomach was more akin to a Buddha belly than a wash-boarded six-pack. So, how could I actually increase my strength, flexibility and balance to the level required to surf?

Tim Ferriss has a clever system for helping you to achieve difficult goals. Write a big enough cheque for an amount that would hurt if cashed and then give it to a friend and tell them that if you fail at your goal then they can cash it in!

Another great tip I learned some years ago was that instead of just hoping for success you can actually create so many supportive situations and actions for yourself that success is just inevitable.

An Olympic gold medallist doesn't just turn up at the track to train once a week **hoping** they will get lucky and win a gold medal. They have a highly structured training regime, a coach and a support team; these actions and supportive situations are all contributing to their future success.

This made me wonder how I could integrate a similar level of support and accountability into getting fit enough to go surfing. As I had no friends who wanted to give up their sofa for the gym, I decided the only way to combine accountability with making success inevitable was to hire a professional trainer down at my local gym.

The accountability part was straightforward enough, every Monday, Wednesday and Friday morning I would have to turn up at the gym at 9:30am to be put through an ever increasingly difficult set of exercises by my personal trainer Will. And over a 6-month period I never missed a session because I would have had to pay for Will to take a tea break at my expense and my Scottish heritage of being careful with money would not allow that!

But how could I make success inevitable? The fact was that I had never even been on a surfboard before, and the sea conditions off the south coast of England were more Arctic than Baywatch.

So, over the months my Personal Trainer, Will, got creative and came up with a whole range of inventive exercises for me to improve my balance and strength;

this culminated in a special surfboard simulator comprising of 3 Bosus and 2 Reebok Step platforms. If you would like to see a video of my workout session on the surfboard simulator you can find it on YouTube.

## Surfing in Bali

When I arrived at the **surf-camp** in Bali in October 2011, I was definitely the oldest newbie surfer they had ever had at the age of 46. Most of my fellow newbie surfers were in their late 20s and seemed bemused that I had left it so late to learn. But my 6 months of training paid off as once we were lying on surfboards trying to swim against the current and crashing through giant waves, your age is not the key but your fitness and upper body strength is. Many of my 20-something newbie surfers just couldn't handle the physical exertion required to paddle out to the waves for several hours at a time.

So, my approach of committing to a regime of daily exercise and practicing the skills required to balance on a surfboard paid off; on my first day out on the waves I actually managed to stand upright on the board and surf into the shore.

Afterwards, as I sat on the beach in Bali, eating an ice cream (a Magnum, isn't globalisation great) after my success at managing to stand up on the surfboard. I reflected on how powerful the ideas were that I had first read in those get-rich-quick books, five years previously.

Utilising the power of leverage to buy myself assets that generated income for me every single day without me having to physically be there; in fact, as I was lying on the beach in Bali I was earning money from those properties!

By waking-up to **The Job Delusion** and changing my limiting beliefs I had managed to achieve one of my lifetime's goals at the tender age of 46 and had not had to wait until I was 67 when I would probably have been just too old to do such a physically demanding activity!

## Back to the big question

Great fun though it had been to finally achieve my lifetime's ambition of learning to surf.

When I returned home, I was faced with the same existential angst of what activity was I going to engage in to make my daily life have meaning and purpose?

This is a question many people face when they retire and stop working, they lose all that structure they had, a place to go every day, other people to talk to and goals to achieve.

Like it or not, we are social beings, millions of years of evolution have shaped our brains to need social contact and if we don't get it, it leads to depression and anxiety.

Meaning and purpose in one's life is as important as the air we breathe, without it we will slowly suffocate and die a lonely, unfulfilled life.

# The Zen of being

*"Always living for a better tomorrow or running from a numbing past, we inhabit this present moment like a shabby motel on the way to somewhere else. If pressed we really couldn't say where it is that we're in such a rush to get to?"* – <u>The Zen of Recovery</u> – Mel Ash

Who are we really? What is the real meaning of life? How can we attain lasting happiness in the face of our seemingly endless troubles?

I was starting to realise that just having money and freedom from having to go to work every day did not make me any happier; in fact, I started to find the lack of purpose and structure very difficult to live with.

Humans are tribal beings; we need other people to feel a sense of belonging, of purpose, of being loved. But our industrialised capitalist world has become obsessed with the cult of the individual and the idea that happiness can only be achieved by consuming more and more **stuff!**

If only I had a bigger house, a faster car, the perfect partner then my life would be complete and I would be happy. That is the social contract we have all unconsciously accepted from birth and it is, I feel, at the heart of **The Job Delusion**.

## Community

The concept of living in a **community** was one I had been struggling to achieve since I left home at the age of 19. I was living in one of those closely packed Victorian terraced streets in Brighton, on the South Coast of England. Locally it was famed for its community but my experience of my neighbours was that most of them could barely bring themselves to say hello and the rest of the street ignored me and each other as much as possible.

I was increasingly feeling isolated, especially now that I had no day-job to go to, no one to say "good morning" to at the office or chat with at the tea break.

Being at home every day was slowly turning me **agoraphobic**; I would find any excuse not to go out. I realised that if I didn't have at least one interaction with another human being every day, I would slowly slide into a feeling of apathy and I just wouldn't be able to do anything productive all day. I would be like a bored teenager that can't get out of bed in the morning declaring "what's the point!"

Then at a friend's birthday party I found myself talking to Mokshini (the chairperson of my local Buddhist Centre) about my dilemma of isolation and lack of connection in my life. Mokshini pointed out that we suffer as humans if all our energies are directed towards our own needs. True happiness comes from contributing to a cause bigger than ourselves. Then she said that they had a need for volunteers at the Buddhist centre to help with everything from cleaning the toilets to sorting out their computer systems. Would I be interested?

## An ancient approach to a modern problem

I had spent my whole life trying to avoid **old Religion** and **New Age Religions** but I had always found Buddhism to be the most rational of them all. No God or higher power is involved, purely a desire to free yourself from the tyranny of your own thoughts and cravings, to be compassionate to all living beings, especially yourself. The primary focus is about taking full responsibility for all your thoughts and actions in the world. They also believe that there is no such thing as a **fixed self**, the 'I' that we use to refer to ourselves or, as Freud put it, this **ego** that drives our lives; they believe that the self is not a permanent state, it changes moment by moment.

This view fitted well with what I had been striving to achieve for the last few years, the goal of changing my limiting beliefs, of changing **myself**. I found this to be a powerful idea, because if I accept that there is no fixed self then I don't have to keep living my life today based on who I was as a child, or even who I was yesterday, as that self ultimately no longer exists; all that exists right now is what I choose my life to be.

A few days after meeting Mokshini at that party, I stood in the shrine room of the Brighton Buddhist Centre in front of a large painting of a tranquil looking Buddha. Explaining to me what the shrine represented was Dharmavasita, her name meant Perfumed by the Dharma as Truth, which was an aspirational reminder to her of what she was here on this Earth to achieve. Dharmavasita explained that the shrine was not an icon of the Buddha to be worshipped, in the traditional Christian way, but a reminder that the Buddha, who was just a normal man, had freed himself from suffering and therefore so could I.

## The three jewels

Dharmavasita went on to explain that there were 3 key concepts (or 3 jewels) at the heart of Buddhism. Firstly, there was the **Buddha**, a normal human being, not a god, just a person like you or I. He had worked on freeing himself from his ego, from his cravings, from his delusions, to find his true self and finally be free of all mental suffering. This is how Buddhism defines **Enlightenment**.

Second was the **Dharma**, the teachings of how the Buddha achieved enlightenment through applying the Four Noble Truths and the Eightfold Path. The Four Noble Truths define how we suffer, and the Eightfold Path provides practical advice on how to free yourself from suffering.

Third was the **Sangha**, the community. At the heart of Buddhism is the recognition that only working towards your own freedom, your own needs, is not enough; you need to bring yourself into your community, to help them become free too.

Buddhism is a very practical discipline, it points out that you can't just believe what it says, you must experience it for yourself. You need to try out their ideas and see if they work for you. Like a lot of deceptively simple ideas, the further you explore the more you get out, and you are thereby encouraged to delve even deeper.

## A noble practice

Each week I give a day of my time to help this small community of Buddhists who are not only striving to free themselves from suffering but also to help others to do the same. I find that I am starting to feel more contented and, strangely, freer than ever before in my life. I experience many people coming to the centre who just need to experience the stillness of a peaceful sanctuary as a respite from the noise of their daily lives. They may be going through a debilitating illness or just curious about a different way of thinking and being.

I realised that my life had been full of suffering due to craving stuff like money, possessions and relationships, and because I had been fighting against the impermanence of the world (the fact that every person, object and emotion ultimately changes). The Buddhist model helped me to make sense of all of this as well as providing practical advice concerning how to deal with it.

I was surprised to find that my new way of living was making me feel rather contented with my lot; something those twenty years of having a job and consuming stuff had failed to give me for more than just a few fleeting moments. And that is, of course, consumerism's main trick. Buy goods and then when they don't truly fulfil you the answer is that you need to buy even more goods, and so the wheel of our unsatisfactory life keeps turning.

So, my journey of the last 15 years, starting with the reading of _Rich Dad Poor Dad_, has led me to a surprising place. I now own assets that generate enough passive income for me to be financially free, and this allows me to spend my time as I choose I still work but in an area I choose to work in without the fear that I _have_ to work to pay the bills.

And the area I now work in is helping others become **financially free** by using the experience gained over the last 15 years and my more formal training as a Financial Adviser and Coach to help individuals on a one-to-one basis.

Find out more at my web site

www.KevinHBoyd.com

# Conclusion

I hope the tale of my journey from my day job to financial freedom, by discovering how the rich think and then copying them by generating passive income, has encouraged you to work on your own beliefs about money and ultimately take action to change them!

Most of us were sold **The Job Delusion** early on in our lives – we were told:

"Get educated, work hard at your job and only when you retire will you be free to do all the things that you wanted to do while working away your life!"

The concept behind that maxim was that when you retired you would of course then have a generous pension to support you in your retirement.

Well, this may have been true in the 20th Century, but the realities of globalisation in the 21st Century make this promise precarious at best. It's a bit like betting on a horse race that takes 45 years to run. Will your horse come in first or will it stumble at the final jump 40 years into the race? It's the biggest gamble of your life!

But the new rich don't think this way. There is nothing wrong with getting educated, a good university degree is an asset, but none of our educational institutions seem to want to teach us how to get rich, just how to have a job.

However, a few mavericks have decided to help us achieve financial freedom.

Robert Kiyosaki's books _Rich Dad, Poor Dad_ and the sequel _Rich Dad's Cashflow Quadrant_ will teach you how the new rich create wealth and freedom by generating passive income through owning or leasing assets. These assets pay you money every day even when you are asleep or lying on the beach drinking Piña Coladas!

The next step is to examine your own limiting beliefs about money and what you are worth.

T. Harv Eker's book _Secrets of the Millionaire Mind_ explores this subject in great depth; it explains that we all have a **money blueprint** wired into our subconscious minds (which means we are unaware of it). This blueprint is the reason why most lottery winners' end up spending all their winnings and end up back at the same financial level as they were before they won.

As we all discovered in the crash of 2008, banks seem to have lost their lending intelligence. They rely way too much on simplistic computer models to manage their lending risk, models that don't take into account human nature. We no longer have a normal human relationship with a bank manager anymore; instead, we must pass through a set of binary tick boxes that decree whether we are worthy of their money or not.

As one species falls into an evolutionary dead-end another more adaptable one takes over. Today your net-worth is equivalent to your network. It is the people you know both personally and professionally you should now turn to, to help you become financially free. The Internet has allowed us to extend our social networks across the globe; through the use of online Social Networks like Facebook and LinkedIn we can leverage those connections to become greater than the sum of our parts. I was able to borrow over £300,000 from 4 friends using a simple legal document called a Promissory Note that I bought for £10 from www.lawdepot.co.uk.

As Tim Ferris in *The 4-hour work week* demonstrates so well, once you generate some passive income in your life you can then work part-time or give up the day job completely; then you will be free to pursue that list of ambitions you have been secretly creating whilst daydreaming at work.

Set yourself up so that **success is investable** by creating strong accountability with your close friends.

If you don't go surfing in Bali, climb Mount Kilimanjaro or go back to university and study that degree in History of Art (that your parents told you would never lead to a good job), then your accountable friend gets to cash that £1,000 cheque that you gave them when you were all fired up at the start.

The ultimate goal for your new found financial freedom is being able to give back to your community. No man is an island and it gets pretty draughty up in that ivory tower, so don't get suckered into buying yet more shiny consumer goods as the path to happiness, the pleasure they give you will be fleeting. Contributing to your local community will return much more to you. A smile of thank you from a person you help is worth more than all the job promotions and shiny toys that your money or debt could buy.

## Work in progress

In truth, I'm still working on all of this! I have my moments when I forget and fall back into old patterns of craving and association with negative thoughts.

I still have thoughts and feelings like, if only I had more money my life would work better, that my life would be easier if I went back to my day job because I wouldn't have to **think** about what to do each day and I could just rely on my boss to tell me **who to be**.

However, being financially free is a Road Less Travelled and although the destination is not always clear you do meet other travellers on that road that inspire you to keep going. These fellow travellers might also show you other roads that are just as interesting.

So, I hope my story has inspired you to work on re-examining your beliefs about money and becoming financially free.

Financial freedom is achievable, it just takes some hard work now and the good thing is that this hard work will pay off further down the line, unlike the day job which will demand your hard work every day of your working life.

So, I hope to see you out there on the same road taking risks, challenging your beliefs and having a blast!

Travel well my fellow entrepreneur...

Kevin H. Boyd

www.KevinHBoyd.com

# Resources

### Dr Jordan B. Peterson – 12 Rules for life

This Canadian psychologist has a lot of wise advice for changing behaviour and taking action. In particular the advice that if you want a life full of meaning and purpose then lift a heavy weight. And this is exactly what I hope I have inspired you to do.

https://www.jordanbpeterson.com/12-rules-for-life/

### Sam Harris – Waking Up

Learning to meditate can feel like a big challenge. There are many meditation apps out there but I found Sam Harris to have the best voice and the most scientific approach to teaching meditation.

www.wakingup.com

**Tim Ferriss**

Ferriss has figured out a lot of the skills required to become financially free so check out his blog; it is well worth subscribing too.

www.fourhourworkweek.com

**Smart Passive Income**

This is a really helpful and honest site on how to start to build a passive income.

www.smartpassiveincome.com

**Property Tribes**

Many people charge huge sums of money to teach you the most basic knowledge about making money out of property. Here is one forum that is free and contains a wealth of experience in the UK.

www.PropertyTribes.com

## Legal contracts

If you need a quick and cheap legal contract and would rather not pay a lawyer hundreds of pounds then check out.

www.lawdepot.co.uk

## Compound effect

Once you have taken the big step forward, maintaining momentum can be challenging. The book *The Compound Effect* by Darren Hardy gives some great advice on the subject.

## Think and grow rich

This is the granddaddy of all get rich quick books; it was published in 1937 and is now in the public domain. Its language is a bit old fashioned but the ideas are sound. You can usually buy it very cheaply on Amazon.

**Bloomberg's – Merryn Talks Money**

This weekly podcast is full of sage advice on investing often with interviews with the very people who run the funds you are invested in via your Pension/ISA/401K/Mutual Fund

https://podcasts.apple.com/gb/podcast/merryn-talks-money/id1654809850

**Thank you** for taking the time to read my storey about becoming **financially free** and I hope it inspires you to take the same journey.

www.KevinHBoyd.com

www.ingramcontent.com/pod-product-compliance
Lightning Source LLC
Chambersburg PA
CBHW070747220526
45467CB00018B/1199